THE JOURNEY SO FAR

SAMANTHA TURNER

TABLE OF CONTENTS

MY HEART ON YOUR SLEEVE

A selection of heart-felt, confused, rambling and often dark poetry. With thanks to my ever-patient mother Elaine, my inspirational friend Chrissy, and my loving husband Darren for believing in me.

NOT JUST A STRANGER

A familiar stranger
You entered my world
We spoke, we hugged
On friendly terms
I wanted more
We thought alike
We were two different minds
As you held me tight
Unsure by fear
Of pulling away
You took a chance
I wanted to stay
The flutter of excitement
The feel of your hands
Your gentle voice
My fear of strange lands
Disappointment, maybe
Lust in your eyes
I was being myself
I could only try
You did seem to want me
Your voice remained soft
But I still can't help thinking
You're another I've lost

FIRST LOVE

I remember loving as I had never loved before
Feeling as I had never felt
For with one kiss, my soul would warm
And my heart would gladly melt
From a teenage dream, you soon awaken
Joy turns into sorrow
Today you cry a waterfall
But the Sun shall rise again tomorrow

NONSENSE

The wind took my hat
And my hair stuck to my lip-gloss
My hat flew down the road
Soon to be lost
I didn't chase it
Even though my ears were cold

GOODBYE

I want to thank you for all the good times
And I forgive you for all the bad
Please cherish all of our memories
And the closeness we once had
I can't accept it's over
That our chapter has reached its end
Just let me sit here dreaming
Close my eyes so I can pretend
I realize now it's time
I'll give in and say goodbye
It's harder than I imagined
I promised not to cry
Time will pass and maybe
You'll look back in regret
For the girl you threw away
Might be the one you can't forget

FIRST ENCOUNTER

A familiar stranger; many weeks had passed.
Again, the looks. The eyes told of a great want and need on
both sides.
A chemistry between two bodies living
in hope of a night soon to come.
Could hold back no longer.
Words were spoken through the cause of a friend.
Happiness but uncertainty. A chance was taken.
Relief and joy on both parts,
excitement and fear entwined.
Conversation and kisses, laughter and
light, mystery, and fear of losing a just
found treasure.
More happiness. Smiles and affection, attraction,
distraction, and proud to be seen together.
Arrangements and doubts. Courage, sick reassurance and
one mind, body and soul living in hope. Maybe two.

TERROR

I am the dark side of your soul
I am the demon without a face
Who chases you in your nightmares
I am always there
Watching, waiting to take you to my world
My voice is the thunder
My face is fear
My touch is the chill down your spine
Feel me, fear me, hate me
For remember I am behind you
Always
Breathing in the dark

BETRAYAL

I'm hurting so much
I feel like I'm dying
And night after night
I sit here crying
I hate you for leaving
And going to her
But I'll walk around smiling
Pretend I don't care
Still inside there is pain
My heart is in two
I feel I have nothing
If I don't have you
I wonder if you think of me
While you're lying in her arms
It makes me feel like screaming
Yet surprisingly, I'm calm
In time, I'll come to realize
There's more to life than you
These bad times will make me stronger
Somehow, I'll make it through
It's too hard to face the memories yet
I'll wait until I feel
A little less fragile
When the pain doesn't seem as real
You want the best of both worlds
But I won't be your bit on the side
Yes, I may still love you
But I also have my pride

VOW

Be my angel
Be my guide
Be my comfort
When I try to hide
Be there when I need you
To wipe away my tears
Listen to my worries
Help me face my fears
Show me love and affection
Protection and care
Please never hurt me
Say you'll always be there

MISSING YOU

I've never felt a want like this
A need so strong inside
I've lost count of all the sleepless nights
Of all the times I've cried
Everything about you
Your smile, your touch, your kiss
How you held my hand and pulled me close
All you did I miss
Now you're gone, I have no sun
Only artificial light
Inside I face the darkness
Of lonely, eternal night

CONTINUE

When it seems, your world is empty
And inside you're full of pain
When all you feel is anger
And you need someone to blame
Sit back and take a breather
All isn't as it seems
Change is always around the corner
So don't ever lose your dreams
Lift your spirit high now
Leave the hurt you feel below
Make a new beginning
Go where you want to go
Take in everything around you
There's so much life still yet to live
All the world to visit
And so much love still yet to give
I know that life can hurt you
But don't let it wear you in
Remember, nothing lasts forever
If you try, then you can win

LOVE HURTS

Love can be an endless torment, but you wouldn't live
without it
It's the Sun, it's the Moon, and the stars in the sky
It's the trees and the mountains
It's the birds that fly
Love. First comes the lust, the want, then
the need
A passion inside you growing like a seed
Second is devotion, the happiness, and joy
You can't let go, like a child with a toy
Then comes the emptiness, the hurt, and the fear
The pain inside, let out in a tear

MEN

Men make you sad
They cause you pain
Men make you mad
They drive you insane
The things they promise
That look in their eyes
Your broken heart
Torn in two by their lies
But still, we forgive
We give our hearts back to them
They take it and smile
Then break it again

UNBEARABLE LOVE

What would I do?
If I never saw your face?
Never heard your voice
Or felt your warm embrace?
Time would have no meaning
Outside the world could end
For in my empty playpen
There would only be pretend
A single day without you
Feels much more like a year
My heart keeps being beaten
By hurt and pain and fear
I'm craving now to hold you
To never let you go
I think it's love I'm feeling
But I'll never let you know

LOVE UNREQUITED

One-sided love is worse than no love at all. You have so much to give and long to receive, trying desperately to fill the hollow deep inside but are given nothing but empty pleasure.
Longing for someone to take you in their loving arms, for them to hold you so tight.
There is only so hard you can try.
There comes a time when you must walk away for your sanity.
Somewhere out there is the right person for you, and they are looking for you right now. You'll know when they find you.
You'll just know.

DAMAGED

I'm a little bit used
And slightly damaged
But over the years
I've somehow managed
To patch up my heart
And reset my mind
To give my secrets
To the darkness inside

There are cracks in the wall
But I've built it high
And the mistakes of youth
Have made me wise
I'm older and stronger
With life still to live
No more regrets
It's time to forgive

SHAME

He made her no promises
He told her few lies
Yet still the flame of hope
Burned bright in her eyes

Why could he not love her?
She was worthy, wasn't she?
For she asked him for nothing
But gave her love for free

For how much longer
Could her fragile heart cope?
As on another Mr. Wrong
She had pinned her dreams and hope

In her pretty eyes, the flame has died
Extinguished by her tears
For she was nothing now, she knew inside
The truth, painfully clear

She went off the rails
No care for her soul
She punished herself
For she was worthless, after all

TRAPPED

The mighty gales blow furious and free
Not caged by time and work and debt
As this working-class existence has me
Tight by the throat, suffocating and kept

TRIPPY

Life is sliding away
Down the slope of time
Now I've no chance to play
Is it the beginning, or the start of the end?
I can't decide, so I think I'll pretend
The Sun is out
Shining on my skin
Should I open the door
And let the warmth come in?
I've got many things
That I'd like to say
But my bottle broke
So, I've thrown it away

NO WAY OUT

No time to be free
While we are young
We are chained to the job
Without the job
We could not afford freedom
But the job costs us our time
We have to work for fifty years so that we can afford to be
free when we are too old to truly feel alive

IGNORANCE

These thoughts like a whirlwind
Full of the debris the journey of my mind collects
A sponge soaking up new knowledge
Then the slow drip, drip of ignorance
As I begin to forget
An overwhelming nagging need to learn
Thoughts and ideas in my mind they burn
A raging flame to a tiny spark
It flickered, it died
And I'm worthless in the dark

DARK SECRETS

The twisted tree
All gnarled and knotted
In the shadows of the forest
The world forgot it
The tree is old
The tree is wise
It remembers what it saw
With invisible eyes
Muffled screams
Dragging feet
The digging of earth
Dark and deep
Silently weeping
Unable to speak
This dark secret
The tree must keep
The birds don't utter it
In their evening song
Too sad to linger
The animals move on
The twisted tree
All knotted and gnarled
The forever keeper
Of the sleeping child

ENOUGH

Leave me alone
To walk beneath the storm
That follows me around
There is no Sun to rise at dawn
Only darkness fills my life
Bringing tears that fall as rain
Longing for the sunshine
To melt away my pain
I sleep within the shadows
In this world of fear and lies
Emptiness is my ruler
Any love I had has died

AGAIN

At first, they met as distant friends,
But time made them close.
Two bodies,
One mind with the same thought.
Soon their problems and secrets were shared.
Touch of body and hands had hidden meaning afraid to be found. He wasn't free, and he knew her view, so, he tried to change things. A voice in her ear pulled her close, whispered what she wanted to hear. The words tripped out; the heartfelt what the words meant. There was distance but closeness and strong determination. She knew what she wanted. Soon there was togetherness, heat humour and happiness, but it ended too soon. Two people. Life was against them. There was emptiness and fear and a heavy heart. Lies and unhappiness, one mind filled with confusion. What now? Why? And the sickening feeling of again.

TRUE LOVE AT LAST

I was ice, cold and cruel
But you melted me
To fluid calmness in a pool
Of your love
A love that is timeless
Never-ending like space
And though our bodies may decay
Even death cannot erase
Your love
For you were born to save me from myself
And I was born to save you from yourself
All we did before
Does not matter any more
Now we begin

TAKE ME THERE

Take me to the meadow
Where the colours dance and sway
I want to lie among the flowers
Watch the insects buzz and play

Take me to the river
Where the diamonds catch the light
I want to paddle in the splendour
Of the glistening water bright

Take me to the mountains
Where the mighty eagles fly
I want to be atop the giants
Who lift me up to touch the sky

Take me to our home
That smells of coffee, cats, and you
To sleep in our own bed, my love
And dream of days anew

RAW

I tell myself we're over
So determined, so strong
Then I picture all the memories
And wonder what went wrong
They say that time will heal
That the pain will fade away
But sitting here in floods of tears
It doesn't feel that way
I pray to God to make things right
Better than they used to be
Silence is my only answer
I don't think he can hear me
Outside, my life seems empty
There's no love to keep me warm
I long to just feel wanted
Now all I feel is torn
I need to breathe in deep
And lift my head up high
Ignore the heavy pain within
Forget I want to cry
If this is love, I'd sooner hate
Hating is so much easier

ESCAPE

Sit in silence
Live in pain
Filled full of hate
With no one to blame
That something inside you
Is eating you away
You just don't feel strong enough
To face another day
It is so easy to give in
To make the hurt just disappear
Take the only way out
Suddenly, everything is clear
As you slowly slip away now
You finally feel release
Leave the painful world below you
And the torture will now cease

RICH

We don't have much to call our own
No need to brag or boast
No money pots or fancy car
Yet, we are better off than most

For I have you and you have me
A love that's strong and true
We live a happy, humble life
I'm rich in love with you

ANYONE AND NO ONE

The old cannot stay
But youth is not guaranteed

DAYDREAM

Find joy in every moment
See the blue behind the grey
Don't be ruled by fear and torment
But see the beautiful array
Of colours that dance
Alive in the light
Creating a story of rainbows
Against the shadows of the night
In times of loss and sorrow
In every drop of pain
Is a memory reflected
But the past cannot remain
There is no time to borrow
Our candle wick must burn
And soon we shall be dust
Then to the stars, we shall return

MENTAL

You have a mental illness, He said
Me, myself, not right in the head
I'm just a bit tired, stressed I'll be fine
No, you won't. You need therapy and time

I sit and cry, the confusion the shame
I'm a diagnosed basket case
There's something wrong with my brain

Overthinking, paranoid and scared
People are talking
They all think I'm weird

Let me just hide. Don't look at me, don't speak
I can't face what I am
Not normal, a freak

A stranger in the mirror
I don't know who I am
Confident, happy girl
Come back if you can

LOVE FOREVER

Don't you dare leave me
We had a deal, you told me so
I was to go first
Don't pretend you didn't know

I thought we had forever
But time has tricked us all
Too busy making memories
Didn't know when we would fall

You gave me everything my love
I want another fifty years
I commit your touch to memory
As you wipe away my tears

This is not goodbye
It's "See you in a while"
Just wait for me, my darling
I won't be far behind

Don't tell me life goes on
It ends with your last breath
Where you go, I'll follow
Love forever, after death

RESTLESS

I think my brain has a mind of its own
It put songs in my head at night
When I want to go to sleep
Words come from my mouth
That I didn't even speak

THE QUIET

Autumnal vale in the valley creeps
Across the water still
Ghostly giants behind do sleep
Their breath creates a chill
Most of life is hidden below
In earth so dark and warm
Waiting for the world to turn
And the land to be re born

MORE

Do not look back in regret, only forward in hope.
This is not the end.

THE RHYMES IN MY MIND

Welcome to my new collection
of random poetry.

I write because I am compelled to.

I may be brushing my teeth
or walking in the rain
when the words begin to form
in my mind.

There is no method
or planning in my writing,
maybe that is why the poems
seem to jump
from one subject
to another.

FORGET YOU NOT

I know you are afraid, my friend
The world is suddenly strange
There is a real threat of danger
And life out there has changed

Do you have everything you need, my friend?
Can I help in any way?
Not just with doorstep drop-offs
Or words through windowpane

For sustenance is more than
Merely bread and tea
What about the laughter
Our chats and memories?

When all of this is over
And survivors come outdoors
To celebrate with family
Not take for granted any more

The liberty and open space
The birdsong and the sky
Maybe will mean much more to us
The joy we cannot buy

The streets will all be bustling
The parks all filled with play
This world will seem much brighter
Through eyes which once were grey

With gratitude and huge relief
That danger is averted
Life will pour upon the world
No city still deserted

But what becomes of you, my friend?
Still trapped inside your home
The isolation rules are over
But for you, it is the norm

For you are old and shaky
Alone since Mary passed
Just a photo on the mantelpiece
You smile and she smiles back

My friend, will they remember you?
Still, watching through the glass?
Will greed and self, return?
Will kindness walk on past?

I don't want you to worry friend
For lessons have been learned
You will no longer be forgotten
Or left alone and scared

Can you hear me now, my friend?
I'm knocking on your door
There's a party in the street outside
Let me help you with your coat

HEAVEN

Come; sit with me on a lazy afternoon
We shall picnic in the meadow
Where the wildflowers bloom

In such perfect idleness
Memories may stir
Like ripples on the water
Watch them fade without a care

Bare feet and laughter
Cloudless blue skies
Warm breeze on freckled skin
The soft tickle of butterflies

Time means nothing here
We are young forever more
For life began and ended
While we found our way back home

MOTHER

As little girls, we sat on your knee
Had cuddles and told you our woes
Played 'Round and Round The Garden'
And 'This Little Piggy' with our toes
All through our teens
And stupid mistakes
You always stood by us
No matter the shame

I want you to know
We have always felt loved
Always felt blessed
That you are our Mum

Now you are older
The children you raised
Will never forsake you
Or the memories made

YOUR MOUNTAIN

Take a breath
Take your time
Take in the view
One foot in front of the other
The summit will wait for you
There is no rush or judgement
Let others pass on by
You are not here for them
Let the mountain be your guide
In fellowship or solitude
We all walk for a reason
United by our love of the fells
Their beauty and our freedom

MYSTERY MOON

I rise early to see the Moon
Before it sets behind the black
Skeleton branches of our tree

The yellow-white orb with an eerie glow
Somehow makes me feel both ageless
And ancient at the same time

I am captivated
This lunar spectacle draws me in
Like a magpie to a diamond
Shining and enticing in its wonder
The Moon shines on us all
The early morning workers
Relishing their coffee with bleary eyes
Remnants of a dream still cloudy in their mind
On the tiny mice that scurry in the grass
Illuminating their secrets to the night owl that hunts them

But this moon, this special, bright, glorious full moon
Is shining for me
Just me
I am alone and the Moon sees me
For one magical moment, I know
I know everything
Then it is gone

SWEET MUSIC

I am hypnotized by your melody
You play my heartstrings like a harp
A rhythm that is haunting me
The distant drumming in the dark

Like the piper in the woods
You lure me in, a trance-like state
I am attracted to your heartbeat
And the music that it makes

NO MONEY AND NOTHING TO DO

I didn't get dressed today
There really was no point
No one came to visit
And I wasn't going out
I didn't clean my teeth today; I forgot
I haven't eaten anyway
So maybe it doesn't matter
If I even brush them or not
I will shower in the morning
Maybe wash my hair
Put on a bit of makeup
But there's no one here to care
Daytime TV is awful
All funeral ads and loans
Cancel the licence
I have no interest any more
Social media
What are all the happy people doing today?
Such fantastic lives they lead
Exotic holidays
Sightseeing and spending
Designer clothes
I'm turning them off
It's too depressing to know
Anyway, I'm tired
I might go back to bed
No money and nothing to do
I may as well be dead

PEACE

Time does not matter
No clock is ticking for me
I can stay here in lazy contentment
Nowhere I need to be

Blue sky above
Grass between my toes
Listening to the river
The ever-trickling flow

On and on
Continuous to the sea
Oh, how happy I am
To finally be free

FAITH

Who is it that I talk to in my head?
Is it you that I pray to as I lay in my bed?
I do not know if I believe in religion
But I do know I believe in you

I asked you for a sign once
To show me the way to go
But when the sign was given
I was too afraid to know

I tell you my worries
Give thanks for your help
I pray you give me courage
Long life and good health

I have never fully read a bible
I do not know the Lord's Prayer
Yet, I feel you all around me
I believe that you are there

Small steps, a toe in the water
I am making my way to you

PLAY PRETEND

The birds are calling for me, Robin, Blackbird, and Wren
Fill the feeders, change the water
For a minute, let's play pretend

Thrown over the back of the sofa
Your T-shirt is where you left it
Socks still stuffed inside your worn trainers
I told you off for being messy

I can lie star-shaped in the bed now
Your leg hair no longer makes me itch
The quilt is all mine
But it smothers me with loneliness
I miss you all the time

The birds are calling for me, Robin, Blackbird, and Wren
I have to fill the feeders, change the water
Play pretend

NOT SO GRIM UP NORTH

Some may say it's grim up north
All chimneys, smoke, and fog
The men all wearing flat caps
With walking sticks and clogs
But on these streets of cobbled stones
And alleys back-to-back
In terraced houses row by row
No sunshine does it lack
Mam is keeping busy
It's wash day for the women
With dolly tub and rubbing board
And clothes pegs in her pinny
Dad's gone working down the pit
Hewing coal with all the men
Our Nancy's at the cotton mill
And I'm off school again
When weather's good and Dad's been paid
We pack a bag and catch the train
Funfair, donkeys, fish, and chips
My favourites are the crispy bits
Blackpool Tower, beach, and sea
Children's faces bright with glee
Sometimes we go to Wigan Park
A basket filled with scones
We'll picnic in a shady spot
Relax the whole day long
Friday night, my dad goes pub

A pint well-earned, he says
I hear him whistling up the path
As he makes his merry way
My Auntie lives in Cumbria
My Uncle has a farm
There are many lakes and mountains there
So beautiful and calm
I'd like to take a boat upon
A lake like that someday
Sail to a little island
From school, I'd hide away
Our street at home is not like that
But we do have fields and cows
Mam sends me to the shop sometimes
For milk from Mr. Brown
There is a big house on the hill
A mighty hall called Haigh
With servants for the rich folk
And a keeper on the gate
I dream that I'm a lady
All posh in dresses made
From satin pink and lavender
Hemmed with pretty lace
I'd walk among the gardens
Just to take the air
Saunter among the flowers
I wouldn't have a care
The only way that I'll see Haigh
Is working with the cook
Or cleaning out the fires
All head to toe in soot

Maybe I'll meet a handsome groom
We'll marry in the spring
A ribbon on my finger
While he can't afford a ring
Or I could be an entertainer
The North has bred a few
Mam tells me I'm a dreamer
To be quiet now, eat my stew

We've George Formby, cleaning windows
Ukulele songs that linger
Stan Laurel makes us laugh
On stage and screen, acting daft
Beatrix Potter, Peter Rabbit
Fame and talent
Up north, we have it
All said and done though
Life's not bad
I have a loving Mam and Dad
I never go hungry
No holes in my socks
Dreaming's alright but
I'm happy with my lot
Doors are always open
And neighbours are our friends
In times of fear and trouble
All help to make amends
Laughter from the children
Playing in the street
Gossip from the women
With everyone they meet

We fierce and loyal Northern folk
Are proud and stubborn too
But even though we don't have much
We'd gladly share with you
So, come and pay a visit
There's pie fresh from the oven
I'll lay an extra place for you
Let Mam know that you're coming

THE AIR OF CHANGE

Summer ends, and we fall into autumn as the colours begin
to turn.
Spectacles of bronze as the trees preserve their life.

Decaying leaves give childish joy as we crunch our way
across the covered earth, and nature's jewels adorn the
trees with shiny delights.

A rush of animals gathers their precious bounty in haste,
for soon the land will be bare, the ground solid with frost.
Skeleton branches create a haunting stillness as
hibernation takes hold.

The whisper of winter, the hush of cold, until the air
changes and the promise of spring once more.

AUTUMN

Death of leaves, early dark
But death of one means life

The illusion of fire brings not heat
But whispers of cold in canopies of amber and gold
This is the season that I await
Such joy does it create, in me

I do not fear the winter snow
Or the silence of the dark
Nor twisted branches of the trees
Who are sleeping still and stark

Curious, my eyes are ever to the sky
Searching without blindness or strain
The stars they are eternal
Only hidden as the Sun does rise again

Here I shall wait
For the burning light to fade
Hiding in the shadows
Of the cool and silent shade

While others may mourn
The dying of the light
We awake in celebration
The velvet dark and I

WINTER SOLSTICE

On this Winter solstice
When longest night
Brings hope to all
Who long for light

Life that is sleeping
Will slowly rouse
As snowdrops peep
From ancient ground

The promise of warmth
And sunlit skies
Buds on the trees
The birth of new life

The winter dark gave peace and rest
Preserving energies for spring
Love and joy for you and yours
May the coming year bring

MY MASK

Skulls are hideous and frightening
Reminding us of what monsters we are underneath
This mask of skin that hides the truth
Can be shaped into any disguise
But peel back the flesh
And there is the proof
Concealed beneath
Blood vessels and lies

THE CONSTANT BATTLE

Fluffy pyjamas, cosy slippers
Coffee, biscuits, and massive knickers
I sit and wonder, 'Will I ever be thin?'
As my hand reaches back into the biscuit tin

Skinny jeans and stiletto shoes
No bingo wings or heavy boobs
I can see it now, me size twelve
By Christmas, I'll be a skinny elf

No covering up my bulky size
Trying to avoid judgmental eyes
Or hiding wrappers in the bin
Wondering why I can't get thin

I can't deny, I like to eat
And chocolate is my friend
So are chips and crisp and gin
I know I can't pretend

That salad is a joy to eat
Or exercise a pleasure
Boobs a flying, two black eyes
And thighs rubbing together
No, thanks, I'll pass it's not for me
I'll start tomorrow. Or not; maybe…

NO AGE

We are no longer young. We are ageing and a little grey.
Our bones crack and our bodies ache.
So what?
Let us paddle in the sea anyway.
Let us have a go on the swings.
Let's get tipsy on gin and dance in the garden like we used
to.
Let's kiss like teenagers and feel skin against skin.
We are still here. We are alive.
And I, for one, think that is wonderful!

COMING BACK

I am coming back to you
When all of this is done
Even if the season's changed
And leaves are golden brown
If summer time means solitude
Alone in gardens bare
My warmth will come from sunshine
My conversation; from the birds
Do not focus on the sadness
Or things we may have missed
The Earth is merely resting
Taking time to deal with this
I am coming back to you
We all just need to wait
To heed the constant warning
Stay home; stay safe

ME

My stomach isn't flat
And my thighs meet in the middle
My bottom's on the large side
Boobs wobble when I giggle
I'm not exactly fat
But I'm definitely not thin
Mother Nature gave me scars
To remind me where I've been
My hair's not poker-straight
But neither is it curly
The process got confused
As I was born a little early
I've a gap between my teeth
And a very small top lip
My waist is only narrow
Compared to my wide hips
I've freckles in the summer
In winter; deathly pale
Laughter lines and ageing
Begin to show upon my face
Green-brown eyes
Depending on the light
A slightly pointed chin
My cheekbones are high
I would describe myself as average
Neither a beauty nor a hag
Just somewhere in between
And I'm alright with that

DESIRE FOR THE DARK

Shine your light upon me
Bring me out from the shadows and the grey
Illuminate my lies and mistakes
But love me anyway
Inside and out
Kiss my scars
Heal and make me whole
Always find me
When I lose myself
You know my soul
Is inclined to roam
Searching for that other place
Where the firefly's dance
And all fear is erased
So, keep your light shining
As a beacon
Burning brighter than my desire
To go

The following poem was written
by my husband Darren
on our tenth wedding anniversary.
He is not a writer,
but he wrote this for me.

DARREN'S POEM

You walked into my life
I knew it would be forever
No regrets, you make my life better

Ten years today our souls entwined
Making our vows until the end of time

Our bodies will fail
But our souls will live on
Deep in the tree roots, someday forgotten
But never gone

AFTERWORD

Write what is in your heart.

Write because
you want people
to read
and enjoy
your words.

I hope that you have enjoyed mine.

THE ODD COLLECTION

INTRODUCTION

As a writer, I often find myself with many random poems and stories that are quite different from one another in theme and style. This happens because I rarely decide to 'sit down and write' that just doesn't work for me. My words decide themselves when they want to be written and therefore, I have a phone and many notebooks crammed with verses and sentences demanding to be heard. My dilemma begins when I try to group these bossy little scribblings into one coherent book. Finding such a task near impossible with this unruly bunch, I decided to title the book accordingly.

SILVANUS

I was once a happy child who ran wild with grubby, bare feet through the bright-green woodland. A carefree girl who lay among the scented lilac bluebells and heady wild garlic, I didn't care if my long brown hair was tangle-free, or if my fingernails were clean. Now old age had finally caught up with me and I decided it was time to return to that lush woodland, one final time. As I was reaching the end of my life, there was no better place I could have chosen.

I had lived a long life, which even though it had included some tragedy, had mostly been blessed with love and friendship. But now I was the only one left. When my husband Jack died, that was the beginning of the end for me. We had met as teenagers; I was fifteen, and he was nineteen and as soon as I was old enough, we were married. It had been just the two of us ever since, and we had been very close. Of course, after Jack's death, my friends tried to keep me occupied by rallying around, bringing me casseroles, and inviting me for lunch, but the sadness and emptiness inside me was all-consuming. Then, as days turned into years, one by one my friends also passed away, as our generation began to make way for the next. So why was I still alive and lingering? I was eighty-seven years old, with an aching body and an empty heart. I was just going through the motions of my daily routine. Talking to myself and sleeping most of the day. I felt disappointed each time I woke up.

The red-bricked Victorian town house that had once been alive with laughter and conversation, warmth and love slowly turned into a silent and draughty relic with nothing but memories reflecting from photographs and mirrors that told lies. I would sit in Jack's favourite armchair by the window, running my thumb over the sun-bleached fabric.

I remembered how Jack would absent-mindedly trace the pink, flowery patterns of the embroidery on that chair with his old man fingers, and how he would reach out and take my aged, mottled hands in his. The love between Jack and I remained strong and vibrant, it never faded like the fabric of the chair had.

What must the neighbours with their young children have thought of the old lady with the wild, white hair who watched them with envy from the gloomy window; probably they thought I was a bit eccentric and that's why they never introduced themselves or asked how I was.

I was tired of living, but I dreaded death. What if I suffered when I stopped breathing? Would I be unconscious before then, or would I be aware that my heart and lungs were failing? Would I panic? I wished there was some guarantee that I could've just fallen into blissful sleep and never woken up again. I was at the age where death became a constant wish and a constant fear. There was no escaping the insidious dread that haunted me night and day, and I just wanted it to be over with. That was when I decided to go back to the forest. It was a glorious spring afternoon, and I closed the blue front door of our house without locking it; there was no point, and let my feeble feet take me back to the only companion I had left. Down the familiar dirt path, I walked, through the pretty meadow of white daisies and vivid yellow dandelions, enjoying the feel of the tall grass as it tickled my legs. Along the way, I cherished the warmth of the spring sunshine on my wrinkled face and deeply inhaled the sweet scent of wildflowers. I took photographs of red admiral and cabbage white butterflies with my old Canon camera, hoping the tiny details of their beautiful symmetry might live on afterwards. How delicate and free they were, content with their fleeting existence. I slowly made my way to a favourite spot by the large old oak tree that stood proudly and protectively by the gentle forest stream with the stepping stones, the tree that had been my friend for all these years. I laid my palm upon his rough bark and said a silent farewell. I kicked off my sensible shoes and let the fresh spring grass soothe and cool my overheated feet.

The brown, plastic bottle of pills in my pocket rattled impatiently as I struggled into a sitting position on the uneven forest floor. I could feel sadness and self-pity begin to rise from my heart. I was afraid, I didn't want to leave this beautiful Earth, but I was so alone. I was so unhappy.

Sitting with my arthritic back against the large trunk of the Oak tree, legs sprawled in front of me, I sat there like a rag doll. I sat there in that idyllic place surrounded by colour and beauty, and I cried; loud, ugly, sobbing that was very undignified.

I imagined shrinking down to a miniature-sized person and sailing off down the meandering forest stream in a hazelnut shell, far away from all the dread and pain. Wiping the salty tears out of my swollen green eyes, I looked up from the soft mossy ground, and for a moment, I thought I must have fallen asleep and was in a wonderful dream. Standing before me on the other side of the water was the most magnificent sight. A regal-looking stag with enormous antlers headed a crowd of curious-looking woodland creatures. His golden chestnut coat shone with a heavenly light and his deep brown eyes fixed upon mine. An abundance of red and grey squirrels, humbug-striped badgers, ginger foxes, silky brown mice, and voles. Every kind of woodland bird, from tiny tree creepers to colourful jays; a thousand more curious eyes staring right at me.

The stag took a few elegant steps forward into the stream and stopped a little distance from where I was still sitting, frozen with shock but not in fear.

"Rowena, my child. Do not cry so."

The strong, reassuring voice that spoke to me came from the stag. He knew my name. I had no idea how or even what was happening, but somehow this perfect creature seemed familiar to me.

"We are here for you Rowena, the guardians of this ancient place have always been here, waiting for you to return."

With a shaking voice. I asked, "Who are you and how am I

able to communicate with you?"

There was a chatter of voices from the gathering of animals behind the stag, who seemed to be their leader, and he turned his handsome face back towards them.
One commanding look from him was all it took for the crowd to return to silent observation.

"My name is Silvanus, and I am the God of the woods. I have been here since the birth of time itself; protecting and keeping this realm secret. The reason that you can understand me, is because I am allowing you to. Although you have visited this place for many years, the time was not right then for us to reveal ourselves. We remained hidden but always watched over and protected you, my child." An overwhelming feeling of recognition and calmness washed over my body like a warm wave. I recalled the many times that I had played under these trees as a child, and when as a teenager, I had hidden deep in their shady depths after playing truant from school. With a little embarrassment, I also remembered the secret liaisons of my husband and me when we were still young and in the throes of passion. This vast forest with its secret hiding places and clear streams has always played a part in my life. The woodland and its inhabitants were my lifelong friends; always there, dependable and comforting. This was my safe retreat from the real world.

"I know what it is you have come here to do, Rowena." Said Silvanus.

"Your body is tired and old, and your soul is weary of

solitude. Banlen the wise sent a message to me, and I wasted no time in gathering the assembly."

As Silvanus spoke to me, I guiltily fingered the pill bottle. "Who is Banlen?" I asked.

"Banlen is the Oak tree behind you. He has been your constant friend and guardian since you were a small girl, keeping me informed of your movements whenever you showed up in this part of the forest." He replied.

I was astonished. Turning around to face Banlen, I could suddenly hear a soft whispering and a low humming, which I understood was him telling me he loved me.

"Oh, Banlen," I cried. "My faithful friend, thank you for always being there. Thank you! Thank you for your shade and protection. I will always love and remember you."

It was at that moment that Silvanus and all the other animals crossed the stream and a golden Vixen spoke to me.

"This is not goodbye, Rowena." Her voice was pure and melodious. "Come; we have something to show you."

The afternoon Sun was filtering through the forest canopy, creating freckles of light that danced upon the backs of the woodland creatures as we moved on mass, deeper and deeper into the great woodland.

Having left my shoes behind, my bare feet relished the feel of the soft green moss and lichen on the ground beneath them. After a little while, the animals all stopped by a large opalescent pool of water. There were flowers of such bright rainbow colours and enormous green ferns surrounding this mysterious and awe-inspiring place. Deep caves led off from various points around the pool, and lengths of dark green ivy trailed over grey and purple rocks. The birds within our group began to sing, it was the most beautiful sound that I had ever heard. Silvanus approached my stunned person and told me to enter the water. I felt no fear in doing this and did not hesitate. As my feet broke the surface of the shining liquid, it surprised me that the water was warm and silky. It was like stepping into a bath of cool but molten silver. I stood still and turned my head to look at Silvanus as he spoke to me.

"You are standing in the Pool of Paradise, and you have now entered the Realm of Peace. Please, my child, gaze at your reflection and tell me what you see."

I looked down into the silvery pool and gasped. Staring up at me was my younger self. My white hair was once again long and brown. My skin was peachy pink and plump and wrinkle-free. My eyes were as bright as emeralds and shone back at me with delight. "I am young! I am a girl again, Silvanus, but how can this be?"

Unable to tear myself away from the vision in the water, I suddenly heard a deep and joyful laugh come from the benevolent stag. Then all the other animals joined in, and I too became infected by the merriment in the air, laughing as I had never laughed in years. I felt so light and so free.

"Forgive me, Rowena. I had better explain everything." Said Silvanus with obvious mirth in his voice.

"You have reached a grand old age, reserved only for the privileged ones of your kind. But now you find yourself alone and live each day in fear. You came here to end your life, unable to bear the loneliness and pain any longer. You hoped that those pills you had in your pocket would send you off peacefully into oblivion and death; You were right.

Banlen watched as you swallowed the entire bottle of pills using water from the stream. Banlen supported your frail, dying body as it slumped against his trunk. Once it was over, he sent for me to bring you home."

I felt in my pocket for the bottle of morphine pills; it was empty. I tried to think back to when I arrived in the woods. I remembered crying one minute and then seeing Silvanus the next. I looked at my hands, not as a reflection but as my real hands. They were the hands of a girl. I lifted a leg out of the water and that also was a young, healthy leg with muscle tone and strength. I ran my fingers through my hair and felt the once-familiar thickness and soft curls. I couldn't help myself, I shrieked with delight! I jumped and splashed as my pain-free body was overcome with happiness. I felt as light as a feather and as free as a bird! The animals all rushed to join me in the water, and the birds fluttered and danced around me in joy.

"Does this mean what I think it means, Silvanus?" I asked. My voice was clear and youthful.

"Yes, Rowena, your mortal body died when the pills entered your bloodstream. Banlen will keep your physical remains buried beneath his roots, forever protected, and your grave will never be discovered by any living person. All that will be found are your shoes and the camera. Your disappearance will be a mystery."

"I expect no one will even notice I have gone," I replied.

"There is someone who has been waiting for you, Rowena. They have been among us in the Realm of Peace for some time, although time does not exist here as in the human world. You will never age or feel pain here. There is no death or fear in the Realm of Peace, and it is always spring. You are free to enjoy this Eden and will never be alone again. Most importantly, Rowena, you will always, always have love."

Silvanus' words filled me with hope but also confusion. I was dead, at least my decrepit body was, and I was happy and relieved about that. But who else was here in this place of wonder and enchantment? In life, I had never known my parents, they had been killed in the war when I was a baby and I had been brought up in a foster home in the countryside. Jack had died from a heart attack in our back garden when he was eighty. So, who did I know that could have died in these woods?

Stepping out of the water, I sat down next to a rotund-looking badger, his black, and white wiry coat a contrast to the bright-green grass, and he handed me a ruby-red strawberry the size of an apple. If only I could describe the sweetness and juiciness of that first bite, but there are no words that could do the fruity deliciousness any real justice. This must be heaven, I thought, or at least it was my heaven. I didn't know where everyone else went after.

To think how terrified I had been. If only I had known! I felt like all the weight of life and death had just been cut from me and I had floated away from it like a balloon set free. All that fear and worrying over dying now seemed like such a pointless waste of earthly energy.

Most of the other animals were sleeping peacefully now, and I laid my head down on the soft fur of a rabbit called Renshay, who had snuggled up in my nest of hair.

A shadow passed before my closed eyes, and upon opening them I saw Silvanus' perfect shape standing over me.

"Rowena, my child, I must leave you now. I will be back from time to time, but this realm is vast, as you will discover for yourself, and I have many more children who need my guidance. However, I will be leaving you in the companionship of all your brothers and sisters whom you have already become acquainted with. I also have a gift for you before I depart."

With this said, the mighty stag moved aside. A boy about my age stood with a large smile on his youthful face. He had blonde hair the colour of straw and eyes as blue as the ocean. He was wearing clothes made of some soft, mossy material, which I realized was the same shade of green as the shift dress that I wore. He may only have been a boy now, but I recognized him at once.

"Alright, Wenny?" Said Jack. Wenny was what he used to call me. "I've been waiting for you, isn't this wonderful?"

We ran into each other's arms, and he smelled of sweet peas and earthy soil.

"Oh, Jack, my love, look at us! We are young, forever young, Jack! And we are together in this paradise." I was so happy and overcome with love at the sight of Jack, but how did he get there?

"Jack passed away over by the apple-blossom trees at the bottom of your garden." Answered Silvanus in his velvety voice.

"When Jack's life force left his body, it travelled down into the soil and was taken in by the tree roots. The roots passed Jack's energy along the underground system until it reached Banlen in the forest. Banlen being the wise tree he is, knew who Jack was, and I allowed him to become part of the Realm of Peace."

Having watched us in the forest over the long years of our lives together, walking and talking, laughing, and paddling, sleeping, and loving, Silvanus and the other creatures of the forest knew that Jack and I were two souls destined to be together, always.

Jack took my glowing face in his young hands and kissed me gently, his pillow-soft lips tasted like sweet honey. A ray of golden light emanated from our spiritual bodies as the love between us shone. Turning to face the water, we watched together as the mighty stag Silvanus disappeared into a dark cave on the far side of the pond. We didn't feel sad, it was impossible to feel anything but joy in the Realm of Peace.

"Come on, Wenny," said Jack. "There's so much that I want to show you." So, hand in hand we ran, through the endless carpet of bluebells, never to be parted again.

BYGONE TIMES

"Nan will tell me the story about how you met Grandad," I asked the kind-looking old lady as she passed me my milky cup of tea; served with a small spoon like she used to when I was little so I could drink it like soup.

"Oh, that was such a long time ago, Emma, and your granddad's been gone for nearly six years now. Though I'll never forget the first time, I saw Tom. He was quite a catch, you know! Go on then, make yourself comfortable by the fire, and I'll tell you what I remember."

I was fifteen years old when my mam sent me to work over at the John pit. I could've gone to the cotton mill, but the pit was within walking distance of our house on Woodcock Row in Crooke Village. Most of the local lads worked in the pit and so did my dad before he died young of lung disease, leaving my mam to support me and herself on her own. I didn't mind going out to work, Mam did her best for us and always had a hot meal of potato pie or bread and cheese waiting after a hard day. Sometimes, if it were a special occasion, she'd make fruit cake and custard, which was a real treat!

Grafting at the pit was difficult and grubby but, despite not being allowed to talk to each other while we were working, me and my friend Annie still had a bit of a giggle at times when we thought no one was looking. We even learned how to lip-read so we could silently communicate.

Our job as pit brow lasses was to wait for the coal to come in from the shaft below, then we had to pick out the dirt and stones so they wouldn't explode when the coal went into the fire. All the bits that we pulled out just got thrown onto the floor so, after a while, we'd have to stop and shovel it all up, or it'd be piled high over our boots! It was bloody cold in winter, we had gloves, but they had no fingers in them because we had to work fast with our hands. We wore headscarves and shawls and heavy woollen skirts which were warm but felt like they were dragging you down when they got wet. Mam said they were hard to wash and dry, those wool skirts. Remember, in those days there were no fancy washing machines. It was all done by hand on wash day once a week.

One cold October morning in 1948, I was eighteen by then, and there was a new lad just started at our John pit. Tommy Fisher was his name. He'd moved from Haigh with his old grandad and lived in Standish Lower Ground now. Soon as me and Annie set eyes on him, we were as giddy as two schoolgirls. Tommy was dark and handsome, with eyelashes any girl would have died for. Even the coal dirt on his face didn't take away his good looks. It was impossible dressed as we were to look pretty, but I did my best to make sure I always had a smile when he looked my way.

That autumn was a real wet one and as I was leaving the site one gloomy night, thinking about my tea and a warm brew, I suddenly slipped in the mud and landed heavily on my backside in a heap. Dirty, wet, and feeling like a right fool, I struggled to pick myself up from the slippery ground. I looked up to see a strong, calloused hand grabbing mine, and my eyes met those long lashes of Tommy Fisher. Like my knight in a flat cap, he graciously helped me to my wobbly feet and we both had a chuckle; once I'd got over the shame. Once he'd made sure that I wasn't hurt, Tommy insisted on walking me home, even though it was out of his way. The conversation came easily between us, as Tommy was very down-to-earth and friendly. I found out he was twenty years old, and he was a 'hooker on' which meant he worked at the bottom of the mine shaft hooking on the cages filled with coal and sending them up to the surface. Tommy was not only handsome but also kind and funny. I was smitten. Luckily for me, he seemed to feel the same way, and our walking home and little chats became a regular occurrence. Annie was jealous as hell at first, but after a while, she started courting a lad from Shevington, so she soon lost interest in us. We stayed friends though and would both dream about getting married and living next door to each other, our kids playing together like we had done when we were growing up.

Life went on this way, and we were happy. It didn't seem to matter that we were poor. We had a job, a home, food on the table and fierce friendships. People stuck together back then and wouldn't hesitate to help a neighbour in need. Our little community up North revolved around the coal pit, the school, and the Methodist meetings at the village chapel.

One Saturday when I'd finished my shift, I walked home on my own, Tommy had told me the day before that he had to stay on a bit later that night. I was tired but content, and it was Sunday tomorrow, which meant a chapel meeting but a day off from the pit. As I made my way through the rusty iron gate up to our weather-worn front door, I heard voices in the front room. When I walked in, I was surprised to see my mam sitting by the fire with Tommy. They'd met briefly before, but I wouldn't have said they were pals. They both looked startled to see me standing there, and Tommy immediately rose from the sofa; I noticed he had been sitting in Dad's old spot.

"Here's our Eileen now," said Mam. "Tommy's come round to ask me something, and he seems like an honest, hard-working lad, so I've said yes. I think your dad would've agreed, God rest his soul."

Tommy looked at me, and I looked back in bewilderment.

"Eileen," he said. "I know I've not much, but I think the world of you, and I've put a bit by so we can get wed if you want to like?"

A laugh of shock and surprise burst from my mouth, "Yes," I said.

I ran into his arms and then quickly pulled away again as my mam gave us a disapproving look.

"There'll be time for all that once you're married. We'll speak to the vicar after service tomorrow and Tommy, I'll need to meet your grandad."

A month later, Tommy and I became husband and wife at a simple ceremony in the village chapel. I felt beautiful in Mam's wedding dress, white cotton with a simple pale blue ribbon around the waist and a chain of daisies in my mousey brown hair that Annie had styled into soft curls for me. It poured down with rain but still, all the families came out to see us, and Mam put on a small spread of sandwiches and cake with a little fruit cordial and tea for everyone.

I moved into the house that Tommy lived in with his grandad. The house wasn't much bigger than Mams, but Grandad couldn't be left alone. Tommy and me had our own bedroom at least, and there was a separate parlour with a pantry. Mam was sad to see me leave, but I visited her almost every day. She got a few hours of work a week cleaning at the village school, so was able to support herself financially. It was decided that I would leave my job at the pit to take care of the house, and Grandad. I was happy with my lot, and Annie would come for a brew and tell me any gossip from the village. Cooking and cleaning also kept me busy.

One evening I was laying the table with crusty homemade bread and thick, creamy butter, waiting for Tommy to come home from work. He always said the delicious smell of stew cooking on the stove wafted down the street as he made his way to the house. I looked at the clock and noticed Tommy was a bit late. It wasn't like him to be late, but I wasn't too worried at that point. I was just giving the stew a final stir when suddenly in the distance I heard the ominous sound of a horn, it came from the pit. I ran outside to find that most of the neighbours were already out. Something was wrong. There had been an accident at John Pit. My stomach sank, and my legs had a mind of their own. I ran and ran, my heart, pounding in my chest until I reached the pit. The rain was lashing down, and I was soaked to the skin, but all I felt was panic and numbness. It was chaos. Men were dragging limp and blackened bodies from underground, unrecognizable, covered in coal dirt and mud. Women were screaming and being held back by some of the older lads.

"Where is my Tommy?" I cried, "Annie, Tommy!"

I sank to my knees in despair. He was dead. I knew it in my heart. My Tommy had been crushed by a collapse in the mine. My darling, beautiful husband. The rain had weakened the tunnel structure, and the men couldn't escape in time. I must have fallen into a daze when I was roughly shaken back to the moment by Annie.

"Eileen, what are you doing? Tommy needs you. Snap out of it."

Hearing Tommy's name and Annie's voice sparked a flame inside me, and we ran together over to where a group of exhausted-looking men were sitting by the sheds. There was my Tommy. Bruised, bloody, but alive! I threw my arms around him and sobbed.

"Easy lass, I'm alright, I'm alright," he said in a hoarse whisper.

Six lads lost their lives that day. One was from our village. He was only sixteen and named Billy Halsall, Mam and me used to see him and the others at the chapel. There was a memorial service and later a plaque was erected with the names of those poor souls who had died. The loss hit the village hard, but the mine was soon back up and running. Coal mining was the livelihood of nearly everyone, and people just couldn't afford to leave, despite the risk. It was one of many mining tragedies that happened in various coal mines up North and even though the mine owners made changes, accidents still happened, and people still died.

Your grandad, Tommy, was incredibly lucky. He managed to get out as he was working near the entrance, but he was saddened by the loss of his pals. Right until his own death as an old man, he'd still visit that memorial plaque and run his fingers over the names. He used to say that you never really forget a tragedy like that, no matter how many years may pass.

Well, as you know, your grandad and me remained in Wigan here in Standish Lower Ground all our lives and had your dad and your auntie Betty. As it turned out, Annie got married and had two sons. They moved into the house next door but one, and we'd chat over the fence while the kids played in the garden. It was a simple life, but we were happy with what we had and never imagined wanting more.

Tommy and me were married for fifty-two years, and I know that he's up there waiting for me with his long lashes and a loving hand to pull me up to heaven.

SPRING FOR
THE VERY FIRST TIME

The Winter darkness I used to
dread
For the terrors would haunt me
then
I was a prisoner trapped inside my own
head
No escape and nowhere to
run
My petals seemed always to be
wilted
All colours around me
subdued
The light outside could not reach
me
From the living, I was too far
removed
I could find no joy in
beauty
Birdsong became only
noise
Raindrops would no longer soothe
me
In fear, my hollow stem
recoiled
But I am tough because I am
fragile
My strength was just buried
deep

I only needed to rest
awhile
In safe, restorative
sleep
Gentle rain upon dry
lips
Awoke me from dark
despair
From Earth and sky, I took a
sip
And inhaled the sweetened
air
The flowers all bloomed
and danced with
mirth
As the clouds of sorrow
parted
Emerging like a second
birth
I arose all joyful
hearted
The sky had never been so
blue
The Sun never shone so
bright
Breaking through my unhappy
cocoon
It was like spring for the very first time

THE ARTIST

There is no artist quite as
fine
As one who paints with brush
divine
With every stroke, they mould and shape
With every flick, they
animate
Imagination knows no
bounds
From empty easel life
astounds
Our mortal talents, dull and
mild
Cannot compare to wonders
wild
Their rivers round and smooth the
stones
Which lie on bed and
bank
Their golden skies ignite the
clouds
And warm the velvet
flank
Of stag who proud and regal
stands
So true in form and
colour

A stroke of brown, a white
highlight
An image like no
other
Such talent that can conjure
life
With mere pencil, brush and
paint
Must surely be from Heaven
sent
To share this gift so
great!

CHILDHOOD MEMORIES

I used to love the summer holidays when I was little.
The seemingly endless warm days and freedom to play.
To get muddy, dig up clay
and shape it into animals brought to life by my own
imagination.
Lying in the village park, bright-green grass stains on
white socks,
making daisy chains that would never last and blowing the
time away on dandelion clocks.
My childhood memories of summer
are always lit with the yellow
memory of twirling
buttercups under our chin to see if we liked butter.

WHAT IS A DREAM?

What is a dream?
Just thoughts from the
day
Jumbled up and
replayed
As a film on the waves in our
brain?
A cinematic slide of the unconscious
mind
Creating nonsense of memories remade?
Do our souls awaken while our mortal
bodies rest?
Do our spirits dance and
play
With the ones, we thought were dead?
But dreams are thin and merely wisps
Of scenes, we cannot
hold
For when we wake and eyes
forget
The curtain falls once
more

THAT CLOCK

Tick-tock, tick-tock
There it goes stealing my time
Gone, gone
With every second, with every chime
It used to be silent that clock
Before I noticed it
Even though I was travelling fast, so fast
That clock remained unheard
Not now
Now I hear it
Loud like thunder, like waves
Ticking, always ticking
Counting down to my demise
When did I first hear it, that clock?
Was it when the music died?
Maybe
That was when the thoughts began
That was when I realized

LUCKY CLOVERS

I found two lucky four-leaf clovers today, they were just sitting there in plain sight. So many childhood minutes, I had searched unsuccessfully through the millions to find just one. Now I had found two without even trying, growing in our back garden among the wispy dandelion clocks. See what treasure appears when we don't mow the grass.

I was quite excited about my rare find, and it was the first thing I told you when you walked through the door. "Right" was all you said in response.

Perhaps your Nan didn't win £800 at bingo when you were little after she found a giant four-leaf clover, that forever after she kept in a clear plastic keyring attached to her purse. Maybe your Mum and Dad never sat in the long green grass of springs gone by, helping you to search and search for the elusive lucky charm.

It's wonderful how this tiny green plant can transport me back to a time and place where I am once again a giggling child, who still sees the world as a fairy-tale full of magic and possibilities.

I left the four-leaf clovers in the ground to live on. However, should I hear the death roar of the lawnmower, I shall run outside to rescue them and preserve their rare form in a miniature plastic museum for all eternity.

THE CIRCUS

In 1930, when I was ten
We were lodgers in a cottage
Just me and my gran
My mother had left to live out of town
I didn't want to go, and Dad wasn't around

Times were tough, but so was Gran
We always had enough, and I would lend a hand
With cooking and cleaning and laundry day
Then, when it was finished, I could go out to play

The fields at the back were vast and green
I would run fast through the meadows
Feeling happy and free

One summer morning there was excitement and clatter
I looked out the window, stood on a chair to see better

Right there in the field, not believing my eyes
Was an enormous tent with strange people outside

Such rainbow colours and bright fancy clothes
Feathers, sequins, and diamonds on show

There were funny-looking men with white faces, red lips
Beautiful dancers doing cartwheels and flips

Some wearing tights with large black moustaches
One-wheeled bikes and many pretend crashes

I leapt from the chair and ran to the field
Eager to get there, I wanted to see

More of this wonder, what was all this raucous?
Then a loud voice behind me said
"Welcome to the circus!"

AGGIE BROWN

She lives in a hut in a woodland glade
Built from tarpaulin and roughly made
Her clothes are worn with patches sewn
To cover the holes and keep out the cold

Known in town as Aggie Brown
An enigma to all, her story unknown

One boot is green and the other bright blue
Picking mushrooms in the forest
Making potions and stew

A hat made of tin foil she wears on her head
To protect against mind control
"From the Aliens," she said

But our old Aggie, she does no harm
She's just a little eccentric from living alone
So, if I see Aggie, I'll give her a smile
Ask how she is and talk for a while
She could shy away and maybe ignore me
But there's just a small chance
I might learn her story

LOST AT SEA

We are drawn to the sea
Like the tides to the Moon
Tethered by some silvery thread

Back and forth go we
Compelled by the Siren's tune
"Return, return" she sings
As back to the sea we are led

Our salty tears add to the swell
Gulls cry above translucent waves
"Turn back," they say
"All is not well; you are going to your grave"

An intermittent lighthouse-beam
Reminds us of land and home
Illuminating our trance-like dream
And the hypnotic ebb and flow

Of tides that wish to take us yet
On mighty crescents of thunder
Washed down to deep and inky depths
To claim us like Pirates' plunder

Sinking ever further there
A violent beauty glows
To trick us to her deadly lair
Amidst the sailors' bones

Unearthly pleasure, this song so sweet
Odysseus, resist the call
For to listen is to surely meet
The death and loss of all!

Sunken wrecks, a prison make
For victims of the Siren
From which there can be no escape
No one shall hear them crying

So, remember on that sunny day
When calm and soothing tides
Seem harmless or that murky cave
Entices you inside

Keep your wits and listen now
This warning I give to thee
Beware the enchanting Siren's call
Or be forever lost at sea!

FLIP–FLOPS

You can't walk proudly in Flip-flops
No matter how hard you might try
The best you will manage is a curious waddle
Like a duck who's unable to fly

You can't walk quietly in Flip-flops
And don't even think about running
With each shameful slap, slap
They're a rubber death trap
And everyone nearby hears you coming

You can't possibly be comfy in
Flip-flops
A thong for your toes is just wrong
You shuffle and slide, causing blisters inside
In the bin is where Flip-flops belong!

ALONE IN A COFFEE SHOP

Sat alone in a coffee shop
Staring at the wall
It's too hot in here
And I've been seduced by the vegan sausage roll

I'm paranoid, people watching me eat
Crumbs and filling squidging as I take a bite
Loud conversations, sighs, and indignation
A snippet of someone else's life

How difficult; do they want a regular or a large?
"Why can they not do a small?"
Moans Carol
"Ask that girl, she looks in charge."

Now the card machine is broken
This has ruined her day
Carol doesn't carry cash
Contactless is how she wanted to pay

I smile to myself as Carol makes a fuss
Her daughter is clearly mortified
I ponder; shall I walk home or catch the bus?
While brushing the pastry crumbs away from my thighs

I finish my latte, leaving a drop
I never see the bottom of a cup
I've got a two-mile walk home, and it's started to rain
Fasten my coat; hood up

COVID SHOPPING

Sat in a café among the brave and defiant
Conspiracy theories and dark looks are flying
She's not in a mask, avoid her like a zombie
Quick, get the hand gel and squirt it upon me!

Everyone shuffling along in a line
Keeping their distance in frustrating time
One-way systems, wait your turn
Eager shoppers, patience must learn

Hands in your pockets, look with your eyes
For whatever you touch you now must buy

Going the wrong way down the supermarket aisle
Head hung in shame like I'm committing a crime

I've forgotten the salad, but I'm near the bread
No turning back, follow the arrows they said

Grab the salad, spin around the trolley
Get back in procession, maybe nobody saw me

No time for browsing, I must be fast
There's someone behind me swearing in their mask
They want to look in the discounted crate
But keeping safe distance means they just have to wait

Screens at the checkout, cash is the devil
You better pay by card or face the wrath of Beryl!
Eyes glaring over mask and screen
"Contactless only"
Shouts the muffled scream

What an ordeal, so stressful and judgy
Never again, I'd rather go hungry!

USED

To only be needed but never wanted
To be treated as a final resort
You think my feelings are reusable
I am just a forgotten after-thought

When you had no one, I was there
I never left you behind
For I didn't want you to be lonely
I gave you my friendship and time

Is there a reason that you have forgotten?
Or do you believe your own lies?
Do our memories mean so little?
Has tunnel vision made you blind?

Maybe I am just a fool
Perhaps I care too much
I believed you would just love me
After all, we share the same blood

Well now I've given up
You will never really change
I have exhausted all my hope
And things shall never be the same

TIME MIMICKING TIME

The low hum of a kettle boiling
Middle-aged fingers dip into the tea bag pot
The tinny clinking of the spoon on cups
Eyes watching the clock

Not quite yet, the tea will be too cold
The sound of a key turning in the lock

The light comes on as the fridge door opens
Pour in the milk now
He is home and the tea is just right

He smells of machines and sweat
His calloused hands with rough bitten nails wrap
Gratefully around the steaming cup

A tired smile and closed eyes as she asked
"How was your day love?"
With a hint of guilt in her voice

I view these images now as they were, like cinematic
Slides of a child's mind

Now it is not my mother who stands by the kettle each
Night, it is me

The fingers that wrap around the cup are still calloused
And bitten, but they are not my father's
They belong to my husband

A memory repeated
Time mimicking time
And life goes on

HERE WE GO AGAIN

Here we go again feeling trapped and restricted
Counting down the days until the lockdown rules are lifted

Not all can blow a bubble or online shop for which to
spend
Instead, the darkness has consumed them
As summer reached the end

Do not let the winter gloom be a cause for fear and dread
We must have hope each morning
No matter what, get out of bed

Let each new day be a blessing
We are here, we are alive
The birds are still out there singing
Open the door, look up to the sky

Put on your warmest jacket
Take a coffee out to the garden
Appreciate the simple pleasures
Breathe in deep and ease the burden

And when the night draws in
Put on the cosy little lamps
Find new friends inside a story
Or play your favourite song and dance!

A GROOVY OLD LADY

I'll be a groovy old lady
With long wavy hair down my back
I might leave it grey or not care what they say and wear it
Bright pink in a plait

I'll be a groovy old lady
In blue jeans and Doc Martin boots
I'll listen to 90s rave,
Drink beer and misbehave
And refuse to let go of my youth

I'll be a groovy old lady
And lie on the beach all day long
I'll sip a dry Martini in my tight thong bikini
And won't give A damn what they think

I'll be a groovy old lady
The reaper will save me for last
Then he'll say
"Come on, trouble, I've bought you a double.
It looks like your life was a blast!"

THE BOUNCY BALL SONG

Most couples in love have a song.
We don't.
We danced to Enrique Iglesias at our wedding; a song that
you chose.
'I will be your hero'
I used to hear it played on the radio when I was at work,
and I would wonder if you were listening to the same
station.
Were you also feeling the nostalgia and thinking of me at
that very same moment?
No. You don't remember Enrique. You thought we had
danced to
'The bouncy ball song'
Then you laughed, and I laughed too, but inside I was a
little hurt.
You are still my hero, though.
'The bouncy ball song'
We never knew who sang it. It was just an advert on the
TV with lots of multicoloured bouncy balls jumping down
some steep American street.
I said,
"I like this song"
and you said,
"So do I."

MY OLD ROAD

My old road, my street, my home
Low garden fences and steps of stone
The red brick houses that all look alike
Mums chatting on the front was a regular sight

My grandma's house right at the top
The wood pigeon calling and the gentle ticking clock

Playing outside, eating chips in a bag
Didn't want to go in, so much fun to be had

Just a bunch of kids all from the same road
Some round the corner and others lived next door

Riding our bikes and making dens
I'll never forget my childhood friends
I didn't know then how we would all grow
That Mum and Dad would change and get old

I'm married now, I have moved away
But that old road has barely changed
Those kids, now adults, live nearby
Their parents still live there, as do mine

That road, those kids will always be
My home, my heart, my memories

WARM CUP

Warm cup, cold hands
Wrapped around fingers burn numbly
Such comfort hides the pain
That will come later, and regret will follow
As it always does

LAZY SUNDAY

No alarm, no morning dread
Wake up late, have coffee in bed
Stretch and yawn then snuggle back down
No judgment here, it's Sunday I'm allowed

The rain is pouring, it's good for the flowers
No need to get dressed, I'll spend some lazy hours
Reading quietly with a pot of tea
And a packet of biscuits, all for me

The gentle ticking clock, the turn of a page
With the background music of the pattering rain

A perfect day for idleness, for peace, rest, and quietness
Breathe in deep and close your eyes
Let this lazy Sunday dream on by

FALLEN APPLES

Fallen apples wasting among decaying leaves
Red, green, orange, and brown
Sweet, putrid flesh feeding the ground

Did I fall or was I picked?
Either way, I'm a little bruised.
I wish I had been higher up, desired but never used

Like the big, confident red apples
That everyone wants but cannot reach
Provocatively bathed in golden dapples from light above

But then,
Those apples don't live on in jam and cake or pies
I wouldn't have had any fun
If I'd been left up there to die

Once a ripe and juicy ornament
Now shrivelled up and rotten
No longer full and succulent
Just lonely and forgotten

ALL HALLOWS EVE

I have been waiting all year
For this, night
Enduring the long summer
Impatiently
But now it is finally here
I am afraid

Before you crossed
Over
You asked me to
Wait
On All Hallows Eve
At the chime of midnight

The clock hands are
Ticking
Will I feel your hands in?
Mine?
What if you do not
Appear
When I have waited all this
Time?

With the thinning of the
Veil
You will step out from the
Ether
My heartbeat to guide your
Way
Then we shall be
Together

We will only have the
Darkness
Before you must
Return
Then another endless
Year
Until I see my love again

ALWAYS REMEMBER

Today I am closing my eyes
Remembering the fear of the brave
As they willingly signed up to die
No matter the horrors they faced

With dignity and silence
Mothers held back the tears
Though dying inside
They did not see her fears

The lads from the village
The Pals and the brothers
Went to fight for their country
For freedom and each other

How many came home?
So many bereft
Changed and haunted men
Replaced the boys who left

Today I am listening out for the cries
For the echo of grenades and gunshots
I try
To imagine the smell of the trenches and smoke
As one after one up and over they go

The terror and the glory
Like twisted barbed wire
Of battlefields fought
By those aching and tired

So, today I am closing my eyes
Remembering with honour them all
The soldiers, the horses, the pigeons, and dogs
Each one a hero who helped fight for us

I shall always remember with love and gratitude
I am here, I am free, and it is all thanks to you

9/11

I can only imagine the absolute fear
Of the desperate souls as the plane drew near
The frantic calls and farewell texts
No time left for things unsaid

Observers in horror from down below
Are shocked and helpless as the terror unfolds
The second tower; the falling man,
Screams, disbelief; they cannot save them

Anger and flames, panic, and chaos
The realization of loved ones lost
In the aftermath, the weeping sky
An entire world left wondering why.

Every year, 11th of September
Take a quiet moment to honour and remember
The brave, the strong, the frightened, the lost
So, we never forget the individual
Cost

WINTER

I put on my hat and coat
Still yawning
And step out into the wind and cold of the
Indigo morning
Where the first imprints in the sleeping snow
Are my own

I feel the breath of Winter
As her frigid kisses on my frozen cheeks
Linger
Then her caress as an icy
Finger
Traces the length of my shivering spine

I wrap my comforting scarf
A little tighter around my face
And willingly I go
Into Lady Winters' cold embrace
I see beauty in the snowflakes
As they drift and dance and sway
Each one, an individual
You will find no two the same

Bereft trees are outlined in white
Their leaves lie rigid on the ground
Almost ethereal like
With a frosty skeleton endowed

A fallen log I find
Amid the still abeyance
With warm cup in cold hands
I sit in gentle silence

This day of peace is almost done
And dark is closing in
Time to rouse and head for home
To thaw my frozen limbs

A WINTER SCENE

The winter sky is dense with white heavy clouds
There will be snow tonight
And we shall wake
To a quilt of shimmering silence blanketing the land

One intricate, unique pattern
Started it all
By falling softly
Followed by another
And from that, others followed more

Dotted among waxy spikes
Are colours of red and green
Though encased in her overcoat of white
The Holly is mostly unseen

Twig-like footprints
Of lightly hopping birds
Indent the unspoilt canvas
Creating pretty patterns and swirls

My warm breath lingers
In icy air for a moment
I blow on my frozen fingers
Trying in vain to warm them

This scene of perfect winter
I want it to remain
Just a little longer
Before it is discovered
And it is not just mine
Any more

MAKING MERRY

Fatty treats and Christmas spirits
My favourite dress, I can't fit in it
Festive excuses and making merry
All contributed to my enormous belly

My hips have grown extensively
My thighs have spread a mile
This body grows more voluptuous
With every Greggs mince pie

I can't resist the Baileys
The crackers or the cheese
I have to live in leggings
Now I can't zip up my jeans

Photos are a nightmare
I'll hide behind the tree
And cover all the mirrors
To hide myself from me

If only I had self-control
To resist all this temptation
To favour what's in the fruit bowl
Instead of the celebrations

Oh well, I'm fat, it's too late now
I'll diet after Christmas
So, roll me to the mistletoe
And I'll kiss my favourite biscuit!

CHRISTMAS IS OVER

Christmas is over, the chaos is done
The house is a mess and I now weigh a tonne
Both presents and food were all received well
But now comes normality and the credit card bill

I feel a bit deflated, and the weather is mild
I long for the snow like a disappointed child

New Year's Eve is never what it seems
And it's just another night in the grand old-scheme of
Things

We count down to midnight
Then watch glitter bombs light the sky
Lovers kiss the New Year in
And we all sing Auld Lang Syne

Falling into bed just like we did last year
Somehow feels different
As we shed, a little tear

For alcohol and memories can make a melancholy brew
If we dwell on should have,
Could have beens
Instead of dreams anew

So, raise a glass up to the stars
Keep hope inside your heart
Fear not that things are ending
As it's really, just the start

ECHO

Wild and free in this green glade
I dance beneath the leafy shade
Between shadow shapes and golden rays
On cool and velvet moss I lay
To close my eyes at peace, serene
Bright fragrant flowers ignite my dream
A meadow lit by amber glow
Honeysuckle, orchid, and marigold

The bees delight, the butterflies too
As undisturbed this sparkling dew
Of morning, spring bursts into being
Buzzing, fluttering, humming, and singing

Cool and clear oh gentle brook
My fallen grace, your current took
When sweetened breeze upon my brow
Did breathe away my daisy crown

So rich the emerald sea of ferns
On hillside swell with ardent yearning
To conquer field and forest glade
Before the autumn brings decay

As morning fades and noon recedes
I sense upon the twilight breeze
A foreboding cloud, the air of change
The distant roar of impatient rage

The storm is moving, racing wild
I open my arms, I feel alive
Eat the thunder and drink the rain
I am Nature and cannot be tamed

Fierce yet swift the angry weather
Swayed yellow gorse and lilac heather
An earthy scent of petrichor
Rises from the ancient moor

Sapphire darkness, petals close
Glittering silver from Heaven arose
All is quiet, silent, and still
Until the sound of the Vixen; shrill

A ghostly white before my eyes
The majestic barn owl glides on by

I feel it all, the Earth vibrating
Tree, soil, energy shaking
Through my bones and through my mind
For I am Echo, Nature's child!

IMAGINE A RAINFOREST

Imagine, if you can, a lush and vibrant forest
Rich in green of every shade, yet untouched by man

A tropical rainbow paradise, a kaleidoscope delight
Made magic by the heavy rains that bring this realm to life

Imagine, if you're able, a cascade of crashing water
Thundering overleaf and edge of Mother Nature's table

Life abundant tree and floor
Flowers bright and fauna glow
Chainsaws, chopping, habitats gone
Ignorance and greed, the disease of man

Imagine, if you can, an Eden turned to dust
A silent, colourless wasteland no oxygen; no, us

A PROPHECY

I cut my hand Today
On a small glass garden lantern, I only felt the sting of
Pain
Once I noticed it was broken
And the blood ran red
Into the rivulets of my palm
A river of fate, it could be said
As into my lifeline, it ran
For there, the blood stopped dead
Congealed into a sticky dam
A prophecy of what lies ahead
Or just a small wound on my hand?

THE BLUEBELLS

The bluebells have returned for me
They know how I await
Their violet-scented sanctuary
To transform this forest glade

Winter after winter since ancient times of old
They silently have slumbered
Beneath the solid cold

Quietly they whisper now
A lullaby in my head
And dozily I drift on down
Into my bluebell bed

Garlic white and anemone
Protect my tranquil rest
The chiffchaff and the robin
Singling proudly overhead

Oh, leave me in my happy place
Surrounded by old friends
Who wrap me in their calm embrace
where I am home again

DARLING DAISY

Beneath the feathery icy blades
Of grass that should be green
Is a confused little daisy
Not a sight in winter seen

Her petals are lithe and graceful
Adorned with a frosty veil
A spring bride wed in winter
She didn't want to wait

Good luck, oh darling daisy
I respect your hardy grace
To fight through solid ground
Where you're rather out of place

YOU AND I

Under the same moon
You and I shone
We gazed upon the same stars with wonder
But on time's gentle breeze
You drifted one way and I in the other

I waited for you under the willow tree
Until the clocks began to fly
Where the dandelions found you
And whispered my name into the sky

You had been searching for me; all this time
Then you found me by the weeping tree
And put your hand in mine

NEXT DOOR'S WASHING

Next door's washing is
Waving at me from the grey whirligig
Trying to catch my gaze
As I look around, I see them
Like pastel-coloured criminals punished for how they
Misbehaved
What kind of crime could leggings commit?
Did they stretch too far up
Revealing that 'camel toe' bit?
Did the cardigan lose a button?
Did the white jeans get a stain?
They must have done something terrible to face all this
Disdain
Did the poor clothing know
That the worst was yet to come?
Torture by hot iron
If only they could run
Just then a gust of mighty wind blew suddenly from the
West
The whirligig spun violently
And the clothes became un-fast
Upon the air, the fugitives flew
As their jailer watched on in vain
A pair of pink panties shouted
"Knickers to you"
And proceeded with their daring escape!

CONTEMPLATING ROSES

A HEATWAVE IN WIGAN

Conversations about the weather are all I can hear
People proclaiming
"The hottest this year"
Maud is complaining,
"I don't like the Sun, but I hate when it's raining
And I can't get a tan
And don't even get me started on snow, I can't bear
The winter when the light starts to go
Dark nights are boring and there's nothing on Telly
I'm not one for reading, not like my Terry
He's always sat there, his face in a book,
While I'm cleaning around him, I wish he'd not took
That early retirement, always under my feet
I've got things to do, to keep the house neat
Because you never know, you know
Who might pop round
To chat over coffee and read the 'Horse and Hound'
That's if this heat wave doesn't kill us all off
It's not good at our age, and my friends got this cough
Had it for weeks, but won't see the doctor
I've told her, I said 'You need antibiotics'
Anyway, I'd best go, can't stand here all-day
Terry will want his dinner, and I've the window man to pay
Oh, now there, that's a job I'd hate
I'm not one for heights, and I've enough on my plate"
At this point, Maud's voice trails off as I walk
One thing I've learned, she certainly can talk!

ADRIFT

Not alone, but lonely
Surrounded by time
Time, I don't know how to fill
I used to look on with envy
When time was not mine to kill
Squandering this coveted gift
I sit melancholy by my windows
Where my thoughts bob helplessly adrift
Lost in a boat without oars

ANXIETY

It's one of those days
I'm having a wobble
Panic is rising
And I'm starting to struggle

I'm overwhelmed
With conflict and doubt
One way is fear
The other, a way out

I'm feeling uncertain
An opportunity missed
But I'm also not ready
And my stomach is sick

I'm on my fourth coffee
And my second doughnut
Mindlessly munching
Using sugar as a crutch

BECOMING SPRING

No longer winter, but early spring
Hope's melody, the birds do sing
Branches still, as skeletons bare
Begin to reach for warmer air

Buds beginning, pink and green
A scene of calm serenity

Underground the forest floor
Nature's children stretch and stir
As wakeful warmth seeps into earth
Seeds, roots, and soil converse

Ti's time to grow, the Sun awaits
The bees are ready to pollinate
So, spread your petals, show your colours
Tell the world, spring is upon us!

CATHEDRAL CAVERN

(Langdale)

Majestic cavern of shadow and shade
Pools of wonder and windows of stone
Echoes of memories, colour, and thunder
Pillows of wisdom, water runs down

Faces of rock observe us in silence
The whistles and footsteps of man
There once was a time before they had found us
When peace reigned over this land

CLAIRE

Today I stood a little longer
At my rain-streaked window
And I watched the array of birds
Behind those wet tears of glass

So many birds
Greenfinch, coal tits and blackbirds
Even the majestic swans
All were visible to me
But my gaze rested on one special little bird
The robin
And I thought of you

COFFEE SHOP DILEMMAS

Here I am, in the coffee shop again
I only came in to shelter from the rain
I wanted a chia latte, but I'm trying to lose weight
So, a flat white it is; not great but it's alright

Alfie the black Lab, a regular guest
Rolls on his back to have his tummy scratched
All the staff know Alfie and he gets many treats
While his owner reads the paper, enjoying a bit of peace

I lean forward
To look out the window
The rain hasn't stopped,
But I'm ready to go

I've a paper shopping bag,
That won't last long
By the time I reach the bus stop
All the contents will have gone

I really need the toilet
But I've quite a lot of bags
If I leave them by my seat
I'm scared they might get nabbed

Oh, the dilemmas
Of shopping alone
I finish my coffee
And head for the door

I see a man out there
With a clipboard and a pen
I know he's sure to get me
Unless I try to run

I really cannot chat
As I'm dying for a wee
But I can't tell him that
So, I'll wait for him to leave

I made it, I'm out
The bus is on the way
I really should be walking
I need the exercise today

But no, I'll catch the bus
What a funny turn of phrase
'Catch' instead of ride
Like the bus is to be chased

COFFEE SHOP LIFE

It's November, already
And I'm here, once more
In my usual coffee shop
Facing the door
I'm waiting for someone
They're running rather late
I'm saving my mince pie
But it's tempting me from the plate
Alfie is in the corner
On his lead; I don't know why
My flat white isn't exciting me
I wish I'd got the chia
There's a young girl over there
With a croissant and a book
The shop is getting busy now
Five people in the queue
I really wanted the comfy chairs
But alas, they are all taken
I think I'll eat the mince pie
To pass the time while I am waiting

COVID

Feeling ill is inconvenient
And such a waste of time
A downright grim experience
That struck me overnight

My facial bones are aching
My lips are cracked and split
My teeth and gums complaining
And my nose has a constant drip

A tickly cough won't let me lie
Upon my back to rest
I'm up and down to blow my nose
My swollen throat protests

My aching legs just won't keep still
The shooting pains won't leave
My head is like a pressure pot
With each explosive sneeze

I hope I'm well by morning
I do hate feeling sick
Staying in bed is boring
So, I hope this passes, quick

DEAR SOCIETY

You all made me do it.
With your inbred disapproval.
With your outdated religions and opinions.
Because of the fear you instilled.
Because of your judgement
I became...
This.

EASTER BUN

There's half a bun stuck in the toaster
It didn't pop up when it should
An apple and raisin one for Easter
Extra special, so Marks & Spencer said

I tried in vain to pull it out
First with a knife and then a fork
Then I realized, in fear and doubt
The plug was still in the wall

I can hear my husband's voice
A caution told to me
Unplug the thing before you're singed
By a shock of electricity!

Once unplugged, I tried again
To dislodge the pesky bun
All I did was squash it more
And push it further in

I turned the toaster upside down
I bashed it with my hand
I shook it back and forward
But all I got was crumbs

My coffee was cold, my breakfast was lost
To the land of forgotten bread
Trapped by the teeth of the evil toaster
My special bun was now dead

ELDERLY

I was referred to as elderly today
'Let that elderly lady through,' said they
The young couple in their prime
Probably thought they were being kind

Elderly. When did that happen?
I was in my forties, only yesterday
It didn't really matter then
I thought I was about halfway

When I get home, I'll wipe the dust from the mirror
I don't remember the last time I reflected
Not properly, not clear
Too afraid of what the years have neglected

How old are you, Nelly?
I lost count when the birthdays stopped
I don't read the papers, I don't watch the Telly
My only outing is to the local shops

Does an elderly person wear jeans?
Because I wear my jeans a lot
Old ladies wear beige, I believe
But mine are blue denim with pockets

Elderly is just another way of saying old
You're past it, a relic, you're on your way out
Just biding the time until you go

Calling me elderly, they did me a favour
Like a slap in the face with a fish
For I hadn't realized my life was already over
I was breathing to merely exist

Well, if elderly is what I am
I will defy it. It is a farce
I'm spending all of my pension on a camper van
And they can stick 'elderly' right up their arse!

ENVYING A RIVER

Timeless river
You make your own path
No one to push you
This way, or that
Over and under
Your current ever flows
White froth and thunder
Shaping pebbles and stones

FIBROMYALGIA

Invisible is my aching head
And body stiff with pain
No one sees my sciatic leg
Or nerves on fire again

The fatigue and fog don't show themselves
For the monsters that they are
Instead, they're thought just make-believe
So, it's easier not to care

Silence instead of empathy
Contempt instead of help
Breeds hurt and more anxiety
Than this damn syndrome itself

I didn't want to feel this way
And some days, I'm almost free
But when I'm caged inside in pain
I request, you do see me

A person wracked with fear and guilt
Feeling useless, old, and lazy
Trapped inside a fuzzy quilt
From which no one can save me

Maybe tomorrow I'll walk with ease
No limping to and fro
But that's the thing; from day to day
I never really know

The truck might hit me in the night
And wreck my sleeping limbs
And only once the morning breaks
Do the internal screams begin

But, pushing through and ploughing on
So, not to seem a burden
Just drains my battery even more
Extending my condition

No one likes a 'pity me'
So, a painted smile it is
I know you feel much better
When I keep up the pretence

FORTY-FOUR

You're only forty-four
That's what the older folk say
Yet to the twentysomethings
I'm near my use-by date

I don't feel stale or past my best
Although no longer young
My skin feels much more comfortable
Now I don't strive to 'belong'

My fashion is my own desire
My opinions; proud to voice
Never again will fear
Or pressure, force my choice

But, the changes carry on
Regardless of myself
People, faces, places die
Or change beyond belief

I'd like to pause the clock
Or turn it back to years gone by
Where neighbours chatted openly
And we lived a quiet life

The village green, the Christmas fair
The strawberry summers of old
I'm only forty-four
But never again will be a child

GOLDEN FIELDS

Arrive, oh tardy spring
I am ready for your gifts
My skin is pale and ashen
From Winter's lifeless kiss

Bring me blossom blooms
To cheer this land, so grey
Scent the woods with sweet perfume
And the Sun to light the sky

Dry the puddles, harden mud
So, I may walk with ease
Among the meadows once again
And lay in golden fields

GONE

I am drowning in self-pity
Because you are gone
And I could not save you
Your pain is over
But mine has just begun

Memories stab me
And I bleed tears

The 'you will never' haunts me
Threatening me with regret
I don't want to fall asleep
For then, I will forget

And when I wake
I will lose you
All over again

GOODBYE, WINTER

Spring is late this year. Winter peevishly holds on, coveting the grey clouds and squeezing them tight. The rain falls and falls, creating a patchwork of mirrors below. Winter admires her reflection vainly. Loath to relinquish her grip on the land, she is resolute in her stubbornness to leave.

Impatient and restless, the Sun rises in protest, sending beams of intense, bright heat to banish Winter and to rally the slumbering flowers.

The trees burst into life with crowds of glorious pink blossoms. An army of amethyst bluebells reach up in camaraderie. Winter retreats, but in one final act of defiance, she sends a spiteful gale to tear down the innocent blossom, leaving a carpet of confetti in her wake.

With Winter gone, the Sun shines ever stronger and a choir of birds sings fresh buds to life. The blossom blooms once more, joining the pale blue forget-me-nots, the glorious yellow dandelions, and the pretty white daisies.

Spring has triumphed and with the battle won, Beltane celebrations begin in a whirl of rainbow ribbons, merry dancing, and music.

HOSPITAL

This is not my life
My life is blue sky and optimism
Blossom and bluebells and Sun
My life is safe and full of hope
Determined to live in the moment
This is not my life
My life is rolling hills and calm waters
Pretending the impending future, I dread
Isn't coming for all of us
This is not my life
Hospitals, tubes, and machines
White foam cups and weak tea
Blue curtains and overheated rooms
This is not my life
So, why is this happening to me?

HYPOCRITE

I look down my nose at them with disdain.
When deep down in the well of my dark heart.
I know.
They are the brave ones, and I am the coward.

INFECTIOUS IMPERFECTIONS

You tell me I am pretty
But I just do not see her
This beauty you describe
Is absent from my mirror

The face now staring back at me
From the photo or the glass
Is plain and rather nondescript
Grace faded like the past

I had eyes that used to twinkle
With depths like rivers deep
Now their light is hooded
And surrounded by 'crow's feet'

I do not see my beauty
I feel dull and past my best
Like a long-forgotten lemon
All shrivelled, no longer fresh

But time is the artist
Who paints the memories on my face
Should I prefer an unused canvas
With my stories, all erased?

I am what I am
To change would be a lie
My outside could look flawless
Just a mask in which to hide

Mother Nature loves me
With my lines and freckles made
From running in her footsteps
Not hiding in the shade

To live is to age
And to age is to die
So, embrace your ever-changing looks
Don't be afraid to smile

Laughter lines are beautiful
Such joy of which they show
Infectious imperfections
And we all should hope for more

KILLER

I continued to destroy myself
Enabling the pain
When really, I just wanted to be loved
Each time, my light grew dimmer
As I lit the candle again and again

I am shame
I am Sinner
I am pretty
I am killer

PARIS

Paris, for me, is only a dream
Romantic visions I see on the screen
Painting images of culture and café's
Expensive coffee, perfume, and Monet

The Eiffel Tower, perfect proposals
Champagne, rain, and doe-eyed couples

But Paris is not for people like me
With my Primark bag and my supermarket jeans
The price of a pastry would make me faint
And designer fashions are not to my taste

So, Paris you shall remain but a dream
All of your wonders through other eyes seen

PRICELESS

A young mum and dad, working class
Toiled eight hours a day, relentless hard graft
Mum as a cleaner, working through the night
Dad down the factory prayed for overtime
They didn't go to college, their parents needed rent
But that didn't make them common, lazy, or ignorant
The couple fell in love and didn't care for status
Instead, they valued priceless things
Like empathy and kindness
Their clothes were from the charity,
They didn't have a mortgage
Grateful for the hand-mi-downs
Until they'd saved their wages
A meal for two of beans on toast
From a tray upon their knee
Meant more than any fancy meal to post for all to see
They went without and tried their best
So the kids could have a Christmas
Under a tinsel tree with battery lights
Lay the little pound store gifts
Mum and Dad were feeling blessed
As they watched their children's faces
The tree, the lights; that Santa's been, all giddy and excited
The children didn't know or care those others had received
Designer toys from Selfridge's under
An eight-foot snowy tree
Their Christmas was far richer for the love and gratitude

Than the family down the street
Whose endless gifts lay strewed
Across the deep pile carpet, cast aside so carelessly
Anticipating the next one and opened greedily
Their parents spent a fortune and drive a fancy car
Their children like to brag and boast
Of how superior they are
Their gifts would cover Instagram, Facebook, and the rest
To show how much they could afford
And to brag of their success
Instead of playing with the toys,
They checked their page for 'likes'
While the children from the council house
Rode out on second-hand bikes
The wealthy kids looked on and laughed
At the happy girl and boy
And nastily they criticized, trying to kill their joy
The kids rode home with heads bowed down,
The bikes now seemed unworthy
And suddenly, their humble home
Was compared to the posh and wealthy
Mum and Dad had scrimped and saved,
Their budget had been tough
They believed they'd made it special,
Now it wasn't good enough
Angry in the kitchen as he's spooning out the mash
He thinks how he is failing as a husband and a dad
Crying into her pillow, Mum lies upon the bed
How can they give more, when they've not a penny left?
The bank refused an overdraft, the credit cards are maxed
If only they could get a loan to pay the others back

Despair deepened; sorrow hung like heavy clouds of doom
But then, two little children
Peeped into the room
"We're sorry Mum, we love our gifts,
This Christmas is the best,
We don't need fancy presents to keep up with the rest.
Their mum's busy boasting, about the table and
The tree
The kids both glued to Instagram, they're all too
Blind to see
That what we have is priceless
And we'd never wish to change
So, come on slice the turkey, Mum
Then later we'll play games"

REVIVING RAIN

I don't care that it's raining
Or about the mud upon my boots
That I have no umbrella
And my coat isn't waterproof

I find the rain quite soothing
And gentle on my skin
Refreshing to my tired soul
Reviving me from within

The blossom smells much sweeter
And the grass seems freshly painted
The forest, so much greener
Now Mother Nature's thirst is sated

ROSES

Roses after the rain
Smell sweeter than before
Just like everything in life
That follows pain and woe

We appreciate their beauty
More than just a passing grace
Once learned of their fragility
Will time now slow his pace?

I fear the answer is negative
The hourglass will not pause
And my petals drop onto the ground
Just like the fading Rose

But, unlike her, I shan't return
I shall not bloom again
Once my beauty withers all
There's nothing can be done

So, moments are most precious things
Don't rush or wish them past
This life will take them freely
But won't ever give them back

SAME COFFEE SHOP, DIFFERENT DAY

Guess where I am? In the coffee shop, that's right
There's a pistachio latte that I think I might try
It's very expensive at just under a fiver
But I'm bored with the chia and fancy a new flavour
Alfie, the black Lab, is sat in the corner
He's on his lead and sulking, staring at his owner
Normally, he likes to roam and goes from place to place
Enjoying all the smiles and strokes, from every passing
face
But, there's a Sausage dog in, who's grumpy and growls
So, Alfie has to stay and play is not allowed
Opposite is a lady, she's chatting with a stranger
Who, of her own accord, has chosen to sit with her
The lady has dementia; it comes and then it goes
She's been coming here for coffee
Ever since the shop was opened
The staff treat her like family, Alfie knows her well
She has her favourite seat, on the sofa near the wall
How nice it is to see and hear, the old ways haven't died
That people are still willing to give
Their kindness and their time

SCAFELL PIKE

Scafell Pike, England's highest peak
I made it to the very top
All three -thousand two-hundred feet

I didn't think that I could make it
My legs are not that strong
My lungs were working overtime
As I huffed and puffed along

Then I stopped and realized
This walk is not a race
I want to enjoy the journey
To go at my own pace

I will get there when I get there
Let the other walkers by
They could rush if they desired
I just gave a nod and smiled

And when I finally made it
The crowds had all but left
The clouds had kindly parted
And the view before me stretched

I stood in quiet awe
Feeling proud but also small
My little feet had made it
And I'd been given my reward

I had never heard such silence
As in a painting or a dream
Right in that very moment
I had never felt so free

SHOPPING MAD

Are you shopping mad?
Said the robin to the girl
Caught up in the sweeping crowds
Of a panic buying whirl

He watched from high upon his perch
Avoiding pigeon spikes
The flashing lights and noisy streets
Not a very festive sight

The busy little Elves
Can't stop to catch their breath
Faster, faster they must work
To fill the empty shelves

"Has Polly got enough this year?"
An anxious mother thought
As if the fifty parcels weren't enough
Already bought

"Another bag of sprouts and chestnuts
For Granny likes them most
I know we've got four bags at home
But what if they all go?"

The pressure and the cost outweigh
The pleasure and the joy
I'm certain Polly doesn't need
Another pointless toy

I'm glad that I'm a bird
Sang the robin merrily
That I can fly off to the woods
And avoid 'festivity'

SPRING RAIN

Spring rain, blackbird lone
Please, a melody intone
Sing aloud into the sky
Bring forth the blue, and if you may
Ask the Sun to show her face
To bless us with her warming grace

Feisty robin whistle loud
Ask the wind to take the clouds
Away, away far off from here
So, I can see the blue azure

Spare the blossom, newly born
Please don't take her in the storm
Let me bathe in sweetened air
As I pass by her beauty, fair

Let me lay in meadows wild
Where poppies grow and days are idle
Send me sleepy by the hum
Of gentle buzzing in the Sun

Where time eternal, or seems to be
A place of pure tranquillity
So, April keep your showers small
That I may sleep in peaceful joy

SUMMER READING

I fell asleep with my head on your book
Much blood, sweat, and tears for you to write, it took
It wasn't that I was bored, quite the opposite in fact
I was just taking a moment, to think and reflect

The Sun was so hot, and I was drugged into sleep
As the rustle of leaves sang a lullaby to me
When I awoke, my cheek as a marker
Had held the book open in the middle of a chapter

THE HARVEST

Nights draw in, despite the clocks
And fields are stripped of hopeful crops
Farmers work into the dark
Before the rain and frost can start

Gather in and gather all
Heed the distant church bells call
Bring your bounty, do not falter
Lay your gifts upon the altar

Berries, nuts, and bread and wine
The summer season has been kind
Not too much Sun nor too much rain
Just enough to grow the hay

Hard work paid off, it's time to reap
They've cut the corn and barley wheat
A time for thanks, to rest a while
Let's celebrate this harvest time

THE NIGHT ROAD
TO KESWICK

I am to the brim with joy
Luminous like the full-beams
On the night tarmac road

But I can't help but dwell
As we pass by blackened water
On how little time might be left

Invisible bodies rise up
To protect us, side by side
And I feel comforted
By their ever-present absence

Away, even more away is the Moon
She knows the answer
But I cannot ask her
For she is but a ghost

THE RAVE

It's 8 o'clock on a warm May evening, and I am momentarily blinded as the Sun shines in through my open patio doors. The uncut grass is long and lush. A peppering of daisies breaks up the green. I watch dreamily as dandelion seeds sail by on the gentle breeze, passing trees alight with a translucent glow.

I've just put out the plate of cat biscuits for our visiting hedgehogs, and I sigh as a large magpie enthusiastically hops over and begins to fill her beak. The fading sunlight falls across the wings of the bird, and I admire the blue, iridescent sheen and wonder; Why are we humans born with such boring hair colours? I wish I had hair the colour of petrol.

The Sun is much lower in the sky now, and the midges are out in force. Hundreds and hundreds of them, all dancing about in proximity. The music of the travelling fair plays out a steady beat from across the canal, and it almost seems like the midges are having a rave. The bats will have a veritable feast tonight, I think, and the midges will scatter as if the police have come to break up the party.

THE VOID

As if on pause
I sit
Staring at nothing and
No-one
The white walls absorb me
And
I almost disappear

In the end
It is the cracks that
Save me
Providing a way out
Of the void

TODAY

It is a blue-sky day with warm sunshine and a few cumulus clouds, floating like ice cream islands in a milkshake. I am walking my usual route carrying an umbrella and wearing a raincoat because it is April. I am acutely aware those seemingly innocent clouds can quickly fall, pelting me with stabbing rain and miniature balls of ice, just like yesterday. So today, I am prepared, which means the Sun will burn, the clouds will evaporate, and I will look like a fool. Such is life.

There is a mild breeze blowing, causing my newly self-cut fringe to stick up like chicken feathers and there is nothing I can do about it. Why did I take the scissors to my hair? It was an impulse fed by the need to change, and my fringe was the only thing I was able to change right then.

It was a mistake.
I look like a mushroom combined with Howard Wolowitz
from
'The Big Bang Theory'

Oh, well. I am dawdling and expect to arrive late.
I pass a sign outside the local church;

'Coffee and a chat today, all welcome' it says. I instinctively know that I will attend 'Coffee and a chat' when I am old and alone. Also, jumble sales and, if my joints allow, probably the Ramblers Association. But for now, I am three minutes away from being late. Squinting painfully, I look up. The sky is a brilliant blue; no more clouds. The Sun burns my eyes because I thought it would be ridiculous to wear sunglasses when it was going to rain.

WE SHALL SURVIVE

Nature will persevere
Through the winter frost and cold
Another cycle, another year
Mother Nature knows

That new life must continue
No matter what occurs
She will not give up
While this Earth of ours still turns

Nature and we are one
Born of land and sky
As nature, we are strong
We will go on, we shall survive

WOLF

I am both
Lady and Woman
I am pretty and savage
At once
The choices I make
Don't define me
I am Swan and,
I am Wolf

ABOUT THE AUTHOR

Discover the captivating works of Samantha Turner, a talented poet and author based in the North West of the UK. Samantha's unique voice and thought-provoking insights are sure to leave a lasting impression. Take advantage of this opportunity to experience her work. Learn more about Samantha Turner and her exceptional poetry at www.samanthaturner.net.